S0-BZQ-669

Columbus School Library
So. Norwalk, CT 06854

HOW TO DRAW
BIG CATS

Grrrr!

Carolyn Franklin

PowerKiDS
press

New York

Published in 2009 by The Rosen Publishing Group, Inc.
29 East 21st Street, New York, NY 10010

Copyright © 2009 The Salariya Book Company Ltd.

All rights reserved. No part of this book may be reproduced in any form without permission in writing from the publisher, except by a reviewer.

Editor: Rob Walker
U.S. Editor: Kara Murray

Library of Congress Cataloging-in-Publication Data

Franklin, Carolyn, 1956–
 Big cats / Carolyn Franklin. — 1st ed.
     p. cm. — (How to draw)
  Includes index.
  ISBN 978-1-4358-2516-1 (library binding)
 ISBN 978-1-4358-2645-8 (pb binding)
 ISBN 978-1-4358-2657-1 (6-pack)
 1. Felidae in art—Juvenile literature. 2. Drawing—
Technique—Juvenile literature. I. Title.
  NC783.8.F45F73 2009
  743.6'9755—dc22

                                2008001134

Manufactured in China

Contents

Making a Start

Drawing is lots of fun and very exciting! You don't need expensive equipment. Use whatever materials are handy: scraps of paper, cardboard packaging, or old greeting cards. Try using pencils, crayons, pens, or charcoal. You can draw with paint, too. Just use a brush, a stick, or even your finger.

Grrrr!

Soft pencil

Start by doodling and experimenting with shapes and patterns.

Fingerprint and black felt-tip pen

Pencil shading

Felt-tip pen dots

Fingerprint and felt-tip pen

4

Textures

Wet a sheet of paper and draw on it with a felt-tip pen. See how the ink runs and the lines soften. Experiment by drawing on papers with different textures. Try sketching in white pastel on black or gray paper (see page 6).

Sketching

Carry a sketch pad with you at all times. Your drawing will get better the more you draw and sketch.

A sketch pad is your working record of ideas and ways of drawing.

Black felt-tip pen with clear water wash and hard pencil

Ball-point pen and hard pencil

Soft pencil

Ball-point pen

Gray felt-tip pen with clear water wash and hard pencil

Gray felt-tip pen and pencil shading

Pencil fingerprint and ink wash

5

Drawing Tools

Here are just a few of the many tools that you can use for drawing. Let your imagination go and have fun experimenting with all the different marks you can make.

Pencil

Watercolor pencil

Charcoal pencil

Charcoal stick

Pastels

Finger painting

Black, gray, and white pastel on gray sugar paper

Different grades of pencil make different marks, from fine, gray lines to soft, black ones. Pencils are graded from #1 (the softest) to #4 (the hardest).

Watercolor pencils come in many different colors and make a line similar to a #2 pencil. Paint over your finished drawing with clean water and the lines will soften and run.

It is less messy and easier to achieve a fine line with a **charcoal pencil** than a **charcoal stick.** Create soft tones by smudging lines with your finger. Spray with fixative to prevent further smudging.

Pastels are brittle sticks of powdered color. They blend and smudge easily and are ideal for quick sketches. Pastel drawings work well on textured, colored paper. Spray your drawing with fixative when your drawing is finished.

Experiment with finger painting. Your fingerprints make exciting patterns and textures. Use your fingers to smudge soft pencil, charcoal, and pastel lines.

12-08

DAMAGED

WITHDRAWN

PRESIDENTS *and* FIRST LADIES

ABRAHAM &
MARY TODD
LINCOLN

DATE DUE

JAN 2 3 2009		
FEB 1 9 2009		
APR 2 1 2009		
APR 0 5 2010		
JUN 1 2 2010		
FEB 2 5 2011		
MAY 2 6 2011		
JUL 2 9 2011		
OCT 0 1 2013		

Demco, Inc. 38-293

CRETE PUBLIC LIBRARY
1177 N. MAIN
CRETE, IL 60417
708/672-8017

WORLD ALMANAC® LIBRARY

Please visit our web site at: www.worldalmanaclibrary.com
For a free color catalog describing World Almanac® Library's list of high-quality books and multimedia programs, call 1-800-848-2928 (USA) or 1-800-387-3178 (Canada). World Almanac® Library's fax: (414) 332-3567.

Library of Congress Cataloging-in-Publication Data

Ashby, Ruth.
    Abraham & Mary Todd Lincoln / by Ruth Ashby.
        p. cm — (Presidents and first ladies)
    Includes bibliographical references and index.
    ISBN 0-8368-5695-3 (lib. bdg.)
    ISBN 0-8368-5701-1 (softcover)
    1. Lincoln, Abraham, 1809-1865—Juvenile literature. 2. Presidents—United States—Biography—Juvenile literature. 3. Lincoln, Mary Todd, 1818-1882—Juvenile literature. 4. Presidents' spouses—United States—Biography—Juvenile literature. 5. Lincoln, Abraham, 1809-1865—Marriage—Juvenile literature. 6. Lincoln, Mary Todd, 1818-1882—Marriage—Juvenile literature. 7. Married people—United States—Biography—Juvenile literature. I. Title.
    E457.905.A83   2004
    973.7'092'2—dc22
    [B]   2004041950

First published in 2005 by
World Almanac® Library
330 West Olive Street, Suite 100
Milwaukee, WI 53132 USA

Copyright © 2005 by World Almanac® Library.

Produced by Byron Preiss Visual Publications Inc.
Project Editor: Kelly Smith
Photo Researcher: Larry Schwartz
Designed by Four Lakes Colorgraphics Inc.
World Almanac® Library editorial direction: Mark J. Sachner
World Almanac® Library editor: Jenette Donovan Guntly
World Almanac® Library art direction: Tammy West
World Almanac® Library graphic designer: Steve Schraenkler
World Almanac® Library production: Jessica Morris

Photo Credits: AP/Wide World: 12; The Chicago Historical Society: 5, 19; CORBIS: 11, 24 (bottom); Illinois State Historical Society: 6, 16; HistoryPictures.com: 17; Keya Gallery: 18, 27; Library of Congress: 4 (top and bottom), 8 (bottom), 10, 13, 14, 23, 24 (top), 25, 26, 28, 31 (top and bottom), 32, 33, 34, 35, 37, 38 (top and bottom), 39, 40, 42; Courtesy of the Lincoln Museum, Fort Wayne, IN: 21, 29; Lincoln North: The Joseph N. Nathanson Collection of Lincolniana. Rare Books and Special Collections Division McGill Northern Illinois University: 8 (top); University Libraries, Montreal, Canada: 7; J. Vita: 22

All rights reserved. No part of this book may be reproduced, stored in a retrieval system, or transmitted in any form or by any means, electronic, mechanical, photocopying, recording, or otherwise, without the prior written permission of the copyright holder.

Printed in the United States of America

1 2 3 4 5 6 7 8 9 08 07 06 05 04